Your Stock Market
Your IRA and
THE DEAD CAT BOUNCE

Explore the environment of a severe stock market decline.
Discover how to increase your bank account
and reward yourself with profits.

BILL OVERMYER

iUniverse, Inc.
New York   Bloomington

Your Stock Market Your IRA and THE DEAD CAT BOUNCE
Explore the environment of a severe stock market decline. Discover how
to increase your bank account and reward yourself with profits.

Copyright © 2010 BILL OVERMYER

iUniverse books may be ordered through booksellers or by contacting:

iUniverse
1663 Liberty Drive
Bloomington, IN 47403
www.iuniverse.com
1-800-Authors (1-800-288-4677)

ISBN: 978-1-4502-6477-8 (pbk)
ISBN: 978-1-4502-6478-5 (ebk)

Printed in the United States of America

iUniverse rev. date: 11/1/2010

Contents

Acknowledgements

The Securities Research Company www.srcstockcharts.com has granted permission for their charts to be printed in this publication.

Introduction

So where do you start? You have expressed an interest and curiosity as you have made it to this page. Here is what you can expect when you finish this book.

You will possess the knowledge and the insight to conduct timely and successful **fire sale shopping** in the stock market. Fire sale shopping is an opportunity to increase your bank account in a short period of time with little or no risk. If you are successful with the *"buy disaster"* concept presented in this book you may become your own boss. You may become financially independent.

This book will show you when to buy stocks in good companies that have dropped drastically in share price during **a steep stock market decline. This is when you buy!** It will be the fastest return on an investment that you will ever see. It will help you pay off your bills and your credit cards. It will give you extra money for yourself. Eventually, it will help you pay down your mortgage or pay it off completely.

The theme of this book describes the environment of a stock market disaster to you. The purpose of the book is to *allow you to enter this atmosphere and buy stocks close to their lowest prices in years*.

This easily understood read will prove that **the Dead Cat Bounce is absolutely the best time and the safest time to profit in the market.** Invest anywhere from $20,000.00 to $50,000.00 or more with very little risk.
There is no uncertainty and there is no guess work. You only have to do your shopping once every four years. You only need to have cash available and to be focused when the time is right. You will be **a winner!**

Now to whet your appetite and get the juices flowing let us have some fun in the next ten pages with a Dead Cat Bounce scenario.

The Dead Cat Bounce Scenario

In the fall of 2007 the Dow Jones Industrial Average index (DJIA) was trading at 14000. The market began to decline in 2008. In October, 2008, the stock market took some steep declines. As of March, 2009, the DJIA index had dropped over fifty percent to 6500. This was the low point for the DJIA index. From October, 2008 to June, 2009, a multitude of corporate stocks would drop to the lowest share prices seen in the last twelve years.

Disaster day is here. You need to be in your strategy room more frequently. Signs are ominous. You have been watching your favorite stocks and you are also looking for *a* **new tide of disaster candidates**. The bad economy has sent share prices into the cellar. Stocks are the last thing anyone wants to buy.

The media has been moaning about the bad condition of the nation's economy every day for the last year. This is now the **third quarter of negative corporate earnings** (three months in a quarter of a year). No one is making any money except for a few well heeled manufacturers. Companies are showing a loss on the bottom line of their income statements. The same situation is the case for the nation's gross national production (GNP). The GNP is the lowest it has been in the last four or five years. The economy is shrinking.

Everyone says, "Oh, my God! We are in a recession!" It is a recession. Two full quarters of no growth, no earnings and no profit is the definition of a mild recession. Three quarters of no growth with losses instead of profits is a real "Gosh, darn for certain recession."

1

The four year oil price hike jihad in the Middle East has begun to soak up the profit in the monthly paycheck. You can count on this recurring jihad. It will happen again. But you are not afraid! You realize that the market will drop when the price of a barrel of oil goes through the roof. You watch the market. You are focused and ready to strike when the time is right.

There are casualties in the stock markets. Some companies that are struggling to limit losses are down fifty percent in share price. Strong companies that still show good profits are down thirty to forty percent in share price. This is not quite the bottom but we are definitely on the way. We are half way there.

As the economy slows, the nation "tightens the belt."
Companies that lose income and sales will cut back on production and expenses. Reduced wages for employees means reduced consumer spending. If the recession continues, then some companies have layoffs and plant closures as their production drops and their sales and revenues decline. Some companies will go out of business.

Workers who experience a lay off will try to hold everything together by refinancing the house or taking a job with lower wages.

In order to raise cash to survive, Americans and people around the world are selling their rusting all terrain vehicle, jet ski, sail boat, fishing boat, second car, vacation home or plot of land. Consumers default on loans, credit cards and home mortgages. They file for bankruptcy. In six more months foreclosures begin to appear across the country and around the world.

You notice that the banks and the financial companies have taken a huge hit.
There is an ocean of stocks that nobody wants. One by one, but not all on the same day they will sink to the bottom over a period of nine months. Ford in July, 2009. Fannie Mae in December, 2008. Some will dwell lifelessly on the bottom for a longer period than others.

You are not deterred. The financial sector comes crashing down and with it the DJIA index. It comes down so hard and fast that you duck by reflex. The banks are in trouble due to the home loan and commercial loan foreclosures.

You remain focused. You identify companies with the most reduced share prices and log them onto your watch list. There are stocks down to five dollars a share from highs of thirty and sixty dollars a share. Bank of America (BAC is the exchange stock symbol) is $2.50. Just a year ago Bank of America traded at $40 to $50 a share for three years.

Huntington Bank (HUNB) is $1.50 down from $60. Huntington Bank traded at $50 a share for four years just a year and a half ago.
Starbucks Coffee Shops (SBUX) is $6 down from $34. CitiGroup (C) is $3. A year and a half ago CitiGroup traded at $55.

The thirty companies that make up the DJIA index were at their low point in March, 2009. The 10,000 companies on the National Over the Counter exchange (NASDAQ) and the other 3000 companies from the NYSE have taken their turns for the low point one day at a time.

You wait patiently. You consult your "Dead Cat Bounce" manual. Give it three more weeks. If share prices slip lower, then you monitor price for another two weeks **at a minimum** before you commit any funds. You watch the market for more buying activity. You watch for an increase in daily volume. You are focused on your five favorite stocks and you monitor their bid and ask windows. You watch for an up tick above the windows or a down tick below the windows.

The decisions and choices are difficult. You wonder if you should you put all of your money in one company. You decide on a plan.
You divide your available funds by four. You buy two stocks. You invest one fourth of your funds in each one. At that point you still have one half of your funds in cash.
You continue to monitor the companies. If they drop lower, then you can buy again at the lower price. If the stocks move up, then you can buy more shares and feel good about the low prices paid.

The news media, the politicians, and the business TV programs are going berserk! They present a blend of good and bad news on the world's suffering economies. There is finger pointing and blame everywhere. Good news! The market is up slightly. Bad news! The market is down slightly. **Blah, blah, blah**. The market pays no attention to the news media. You continue to watch the prices for an up tick and a volume increase.

You watch the Ten Most Active Stocks (out of 3,000) on the New York Stock Exchange (NYSE) and the Ten Most Active Stocks (out of 10,000) on the National Over the Counter Exchange (NASDAQ). The business section of the paper prints the Most Active Traded stocks on the NYSE and the NASDAQ. These ten companies had the largest number of shares that traded on the exchange. These companies are **possibly** the most sought after by investors. You check the stocks to see which ones are holding up or advancing.

In your strategy room on your wall and in a three ring loose leaf binder you have a list of the "Top 25 Internet Stocks" and the "Favorite 25 Companies in America." You cut them out of the financial section in USA Today. There is another list of the "Top 25 High Tech Stocks" in the country from your local newspaper.
Texas Instruments (TXN) is one of the best liked companies in the "Top 25 High Tech Corporations." You like it. It is in the black and still turning a great profit every month. TXN is a well heeled manufacturer. It is also one of the top defense contractors. The shares are trading at $14 a share down from $37. The shares are low enough to buy. This may be the low point. You decide to spend twenty five percent of available funds on TXN. You go to the discount brokerage web site and arrange a buy order. With the simple click of a mouse the order is placed all of the way to the NYSE exchange trading floor.

You notice that CitiGroup traded **on thin ice** for one month at $3 a share. The NYSE floor brokers dropped it to $1. This is a whopping sixty six percent from $3 to $1. CitiGroup was trading in the Ten Most Active and it fell to a $1 a share.

You laugh, "Ha! It serves them right!" Even kings of old and loan sharks from New England did not charge as much interest as CitiGroup. Then CitiGroup up ticked out of that window to a new window. Now it is in a trading range fifty cents higher. A positive upward rebound is a good sign. You go to your discount broker's web page and place an order for $5,000 of CitiGroup. The second week it closes up at $1.75 per share. The next week it does not drop back down. In the third week it is over $2 and by the fourth week it is back at $3. CitiGroup is in 140 nations in the world. Buyers are scooping up Citi! The volume has picked up.

BANK OF AMERICA CORPORATION (BAC)

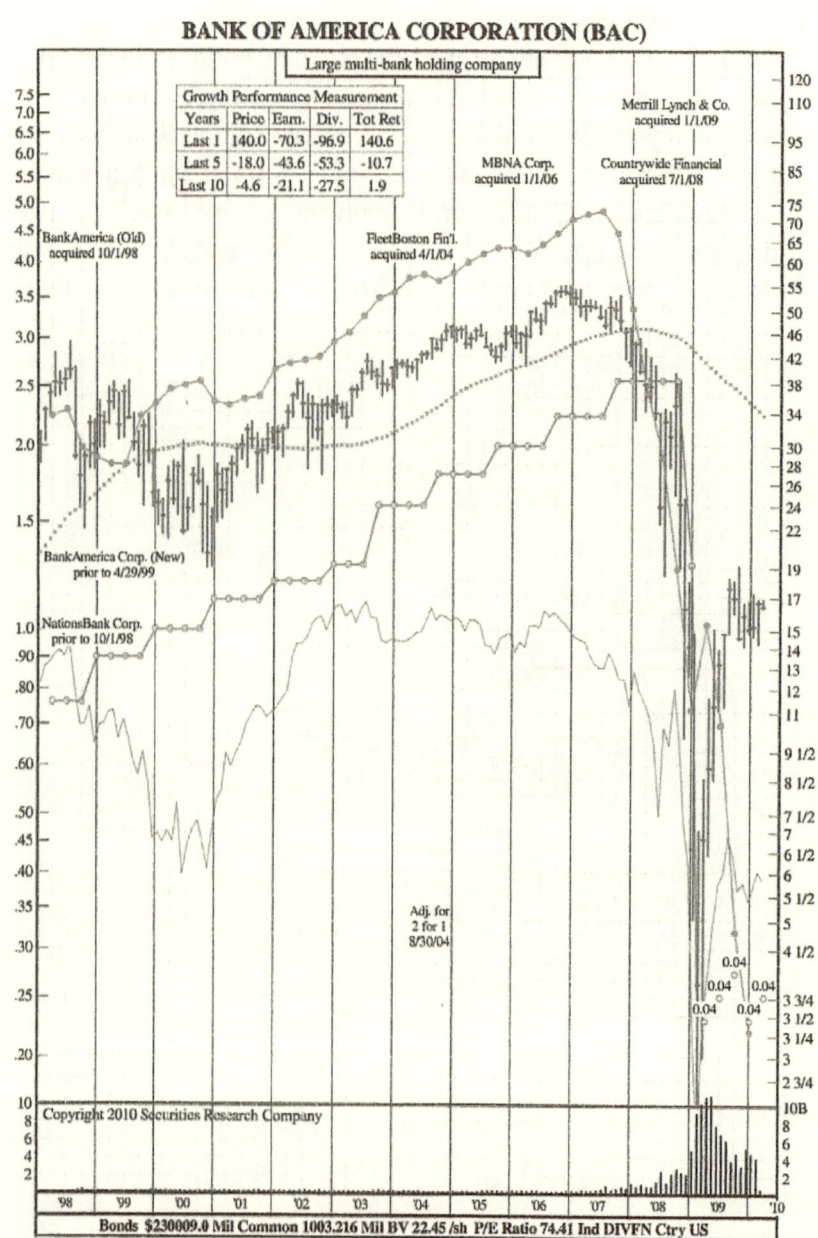

Bank of America Corporation

CITIGROUP INC (C)

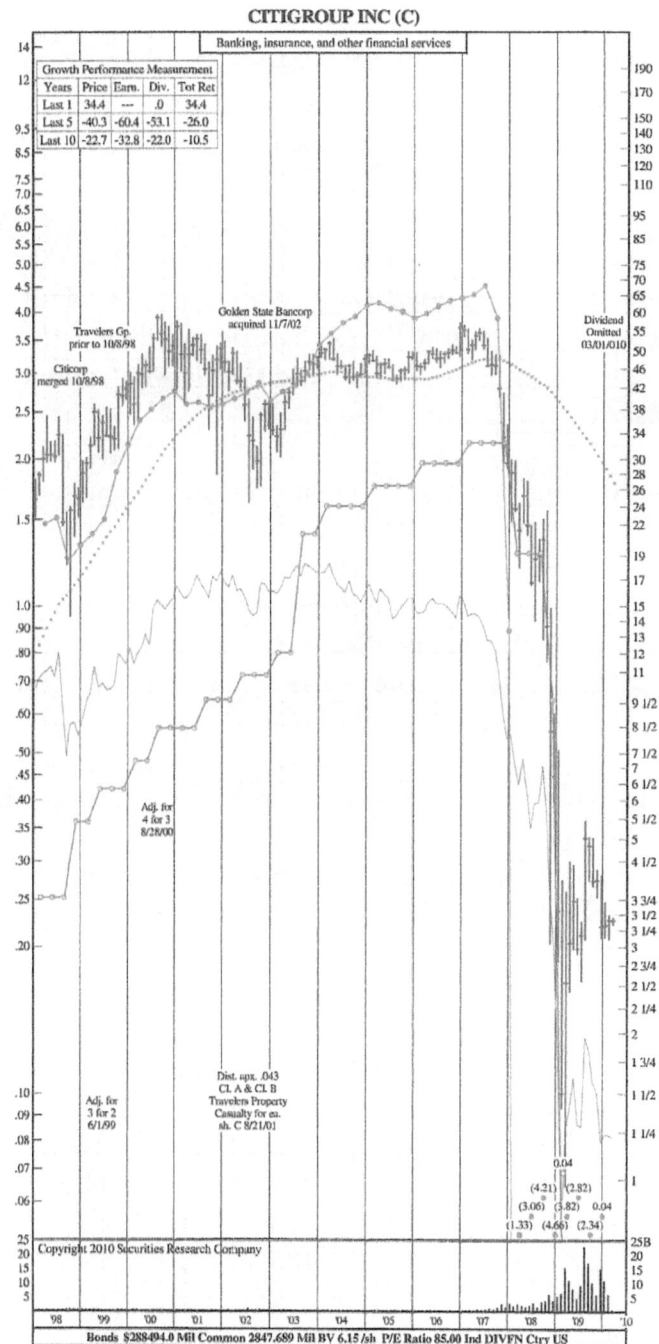

Banking, insurance, and other financial services

Growth Performance Measurement			
Years	Price	Earn.	Div.	Tot Ret
Last 1	34.4	---	.0	34.4
Last 5	-40.3	-60.4	-53.1	-26.0
Last 10	-22.7	-32.8	-22.0	-10.5

Travelers Gp.
prior to 10/8/98

Citicorp
merged 10/8/98

Golden State Bancorp
acquired 11/7/02

Dividend
Omitted
03/01/010

Adj. for
4 for 3
8/28/00

Adj. for
3 for 2
6/1/99

Dist. apx. .043
Cl. A & Cl B
Travelers Property
Casualty for ea.
sh. C 8/21/01

0.04
(4.21) (2.82)
(3.06) (3.82) 0.04
(1.33) (4.66) (2.34)

| '98 | '99 | '00 | '01 | '02 | '03 | '04 | '05 | '06 | '07 | '08 | '09 | '10 |

Bonds $288494.0 Mil Common 2847.689 Mil BV 6.15 /sh P/E Ratio 85.00 Ind DIVFN Ctry US

CitiGroup

On the NYSE Bank of America Corporation (BAC) has been trading in the top ten most active every day for two weeks at $3 a share. Somebody likes it! You consult the Securities Research Company chart book and note that just two years ago BAC was $50 in October of 2007. You look in the USA Today and BAC is listed in the "Twenty Five Most Popular" companies in the United States of America. How can this be? **The bank industry is in the tank!** These conflicting pieces of information are burning a hole in your head! You have personally suffered from the usurious rates those felons charge! **And that is why you buy it! You buy disaster!**

"The Devil!" you scream. "It should be trading at $6.66!" This premonition compels you to immediately log on to the discount broker web page. You log in and place twenty five percent of your available funds into BAC. You buy 2,000 shares of Bank of America at $3 for a total cost of $6,000. **You buy disaster!** In a year or two BAC will be back up at $25. At $20 a share you would have $40,000! After taxes you would be able to pay down the home mortgage.

You ponder this thought and realize that you won! You caught the Dead Cat Bounce! You rise from your chair. Your arms and hands are in the air as you dance at the strategy table. **"Oh, yes! Me and the Devil!"** Your wife looks at you as if you are not the same man she married.

BAC recovered to $17.50 a share by August, 2009.

You missed Ford Motor Company. You snicker as you recall these terrible things you said during your younger years. "Found On Road in Ditch. Fix Or Repair Daily." In July 2007, Ford shares traded at $7 down from $60. Ford has been as low as $2.50 in October, 2008. **The bargain basement fire sale share price was $1 to $1.65 in November, 2008.**

Ford recovered to $9 in December 2009.

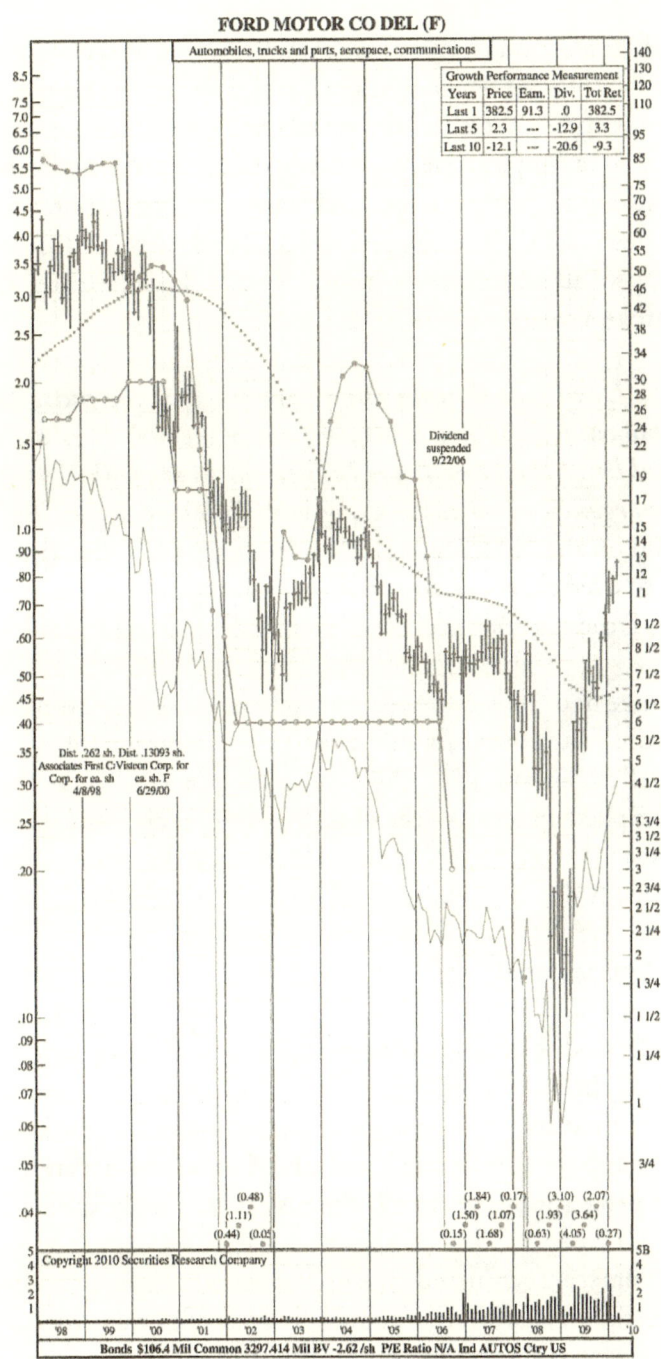

FORD MOTOR CO DEL (F)

Automobiles, trucks and parts, aerospace, communications

Growth Performance Measurement				
Years	Price	Earn.	Div.	Tot Ret
Last 1	382.5	91.3	.0	382.5
Last 5	2.3	---	-12.9	3.3
Last 10	-12.1	---	-20.6	-9.3

Dividend
suspended
9/22/06

Dist. .262 sh. Dist. .13093 sh.
Associates First C;Visteon Corp. for
Corp. for ea. sh   ea. sh. F
4/8/98   6/29/00

(0.48)
(1.11)
(0.44)   (0.05)

(1.84)   (0.17)   (3.10)   (2.07)
(1.50)   (1.07)   (1.93)   (3.64)
(0.15)   (1.68)   (0.63)   (4.05)   (0.27)

Bonds $106.4 Mil Common 3297.414 Mil BV -2.62 /sh P/E Ratio N/A Ind AUTOS Ctry US

Ford Motor Company

Be careful. You are on thin ice here. Stocks have dropped from $20 or more per share to $3. There is still a problem at this price range. It is very easy for these shares to fall another fifty percent. CitiGroup was down to $3 for a couple of weeks. It **dropped another sixty six percent to $1**. It held at $1 for two weeks and began to move back towards $3. Ford had been at $5. Ford dropped to $2.50 and then to $1 in 60 days. Ford dropped fifty percent two times in sixty days. Be careful. **Thin ice can break twice**.

This is the Dead Cat Bounce environment. It is the pulse beat on a heart monitor. It is not a blip up every second. It is a straight horizontal line. The Dow Jones Industrial Average (DJIA) *is dead on the emergency room table* along with 3000 stocks on the NYSE and 10,000 on the NASDAQ. Share prices have fallen drastically. The market is so oversold that share prices actually bounce up slightly. Thus the name, Dead Cat Bounce.

The exchange floor traders are required by market rule to drop the price of stocks until buyers are found. This is the reason for the "free fall." The free fall wipes out all of the good until cancelled orders and sell limit orders piled up on all of the desks and computers. No orderly price decline exists if there are no buyers. Prices drop like water going over Niagra Falls. If the shares have to fall to a dollar then it will happen.

The evil deed is done!

After the electrode paddles have been applied, the shares bounce up like a new blip on the heart monitor pulse line. The bargain hunters are back. Historically they are a mixture of tightwads, mutual fund managers, greed mongers, treasure hunters and **all of them are astute bargain basement price shoppers.** This is the easy way to make money.

New investors scamper in and take up the bargain buying opportunity. Others reel as they have been financially set back or destroyed. Some lose their entire savings, maybe even their livelihood. As you know, every dark storm has a cloud with a silver lining. The young can jump in and pursue their new livelihood. The elders had their chance but did nothing with it. The young look at the catastrophe and view it as the fault of the older generation. How could they let this happen?

This is it! This is **disaster** in the market! **This is the safest time to invest!**

At this point we have to leave the Dead Cat Bounce scenario in order to discuss two important investment concepts, the four year business cycle and the greater fool theory.

The 4 Year Business Cycle

The goal of this book is to introduce new investors to the stock market. The language used is non technical so that concepts and theories can be easily understood. Most of the discussion in this book is **based upon the assumption** of the **four year business cycle**.

Basically the cycle is a simple model of production output. Production is stepped up for two years in response to an initial increase of a public demand for more goods and services.
After two years if the demand is met, then production will taper off and decrease over two years. Production will return to the original level of output. Two years up. Two years down. Simple.

In relation to an increase in production for two years, revenues and sales will go up for two years. They will level off and eventually decline to the original level.

Share price of stock is related to revenues and sales. With an increase in revenue and sales for two years the share price of stock will increase. With a decrease in revenue and sales for two years the share price of stock will decrease.

In other words, if there is an increase for goods and services, then over a period of four years the economy (the Gross National Product) and the stock market will expand in years one and two. Given that the demand for the additional increase has been met and that there is no further increase in demand, then the economy and stock market will contract in year three and four.

From 1965 to 1985 the DJIA index does mirror a four year cycle of two years up and two years down.

In the real world things are not that clear.

As the economy expands to a new level of production, it may hold that new level of production activity if demand for additional goods and services remains. The economy may continue to expand further for another year or two before demand for goods and services levels off or decreases.

The baby boom after World War II fueled a ten year economic expansion of goods and services.

Occasionally one industry may see continued expansion while other industries level off.

The share price of companies in that industry will continue to rise if sales and revenue increase. The others will hold or decline.

The same is true for one particular company. If one company has an innovation or a new gizmo, then that company will grow when the new product is in great demand. It will outperform the competition.

If you own stock in one of these companies, you must remember that the share price will still drop in a market downturn. It will not drop as far as other companies as long as sales and revenues continue to outperform the competition. The share price is merely dragged down with the market slide, but the shares will rebound faster than the competitors.

Companies that turn out enormous volumes of product and merchandise will experience a thirty five to fifty percent drop in share price. Their revenues stay high because they are power houses. These shares recover fast.

Companies that do not have the leading product will feel a squeeze in sales and revenues.

These companies may be down fifty to seventy percent in share price.

They will be operating at a break even point. Their production and operations expense will consume the sales and revenue income.
A few companies will not have any earnings during this period. They will be operating at a loss and surviving on income from last year.

Some shares drop seventy to ninety percent in share price for no reason. They have no following. They are not favorites. Fire sale shoppers are more concerned about other companies.

Companies that are struggling to survive will drop seventy to ninety percent in share price. The size of the company is not a factor.
Massive cuts in consumer spending (from coast to coast and around the world) over a long recession will dry up sales and revenues. As a result some companies are forced to make drastic cost cutting measures (worker layoffs and plant closings) to keep operations intact.
These are viable concerns that react rapidly to change in order to remain in operation and stay solvent. Operating profits may be fifty percent or less compared to two years ago.
The company will survive. They may make a profit on operations, but the company is only half of what it used to be. The share price may be slow to recover.

If the prospect of going out of business is imminent, then there will not be a Dead Cat Bounce. If they manage to stay in business, then the share price will be the last to move. It will be a dog. It may be the last stock out of 13,000 to move up.

Do not confuse net income with operating and manufacturing income. Sales and revenues less operating and production expense result in operating income.
Net income is the very end result after the subtraction of administrative expenses and taxes payable from income. **In addition,** there is the **current portion** of the **long term liabilities debt** of bond interest payable, bonds payable, dividends payable and bank loans payable. All have to be subtracted from income. These current obligations may be so large that net income could actually be an enormous loss.

The Greater Fool Theory

Is the market a gamble? Yes it is! You better know what you are doing.

The Dead Cat Bounce makes assumptions and generalizations to facilitate learning.
The bottom triangle represents all of the buyers and holders of the **outstanding shares** of **one company** from disaster day to the top price this share will reach in the next market peak.

As you near the $8 to $10 peak you invert the triangle. The upside down triangle on top represents all of the investors who want to sell at $8 to $10 dollars a share.

This illustration should remind you of the selling pressure that exists as share prices climb higher. Selling pressure is ever present. There is not enough room at the top for everyone to sell at $8 to $10 a share as there are **no more buyers left**. The peak can not sustain the amount of sellers and the price will drop back to $2 where everyone will become a buyer again.

This illustration is elementary: however, it has a large visual impact. The illustration is used to convey the idea that selling pressure exists and that it exists in a big way. Selling pressure is ever present. Are you a buyer or a seller? You are both!

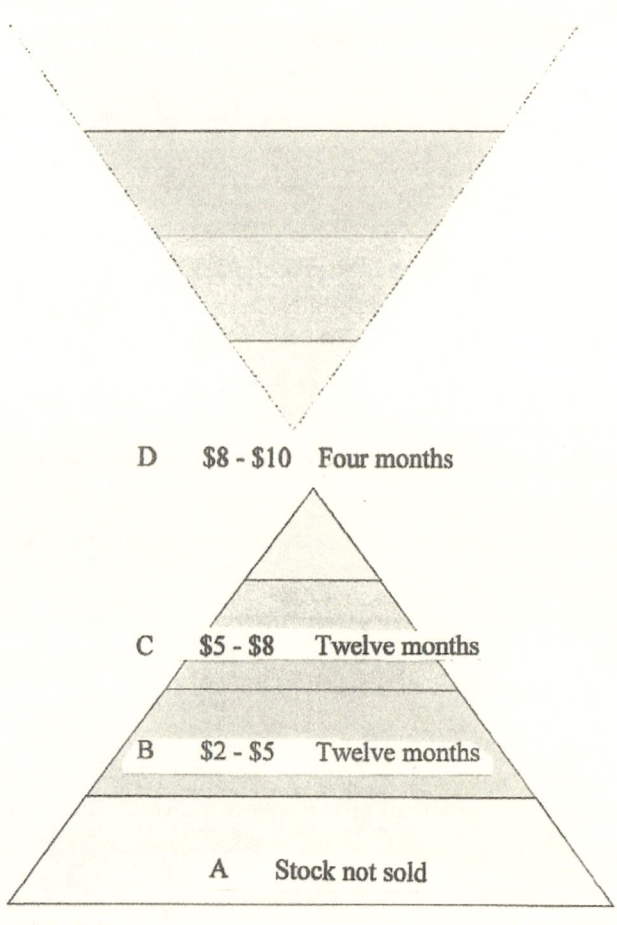

D $8 - $10   Four months

C $5 - $8   Twelve months

B $2 - $5   Twelve months

A   Stock not sold

Selling Pressure

Area A represents nine types of investors.

- **It represents those shares that were not sold in area D during the last market peak.**
- **It represents shares that are paid for and left in the market to ride the tide.**
- It represents common shares of corporations that have been contributed to employee IRA retirement accounts.
- It represents inheritance and trust funds.
- It represents the shares of mutual fund positions.
- It represents shares that are owned by other corporations and investors who for one reason or another have no desire to sell the stock.

- It represents positions required to be a major shareholder. One is required to own five percent or more shares of the company's outstanding stock in order to be a major shareholder.
- It represents stock that has been awarded to managers, executives, and CEOs.
- Rule 144 stock or any stock with restrictive selling provisions and holding requirements over a period of time.

Area B reflects the lowest share prices achieved in the last market disaster. It represents the **fire sale shoppers** and the bargain hunters. These are the first brave souls to jump into the fray of the disaster. Assume the share price is between $2 and $5 in Area B. This price range begins with the first month of the disaster and it lasts for twelve months. **It would be terrific if your IRA employer contribution is during Area B and not during Area D!**

Area C indicates the number of shares purchased between $5 and $8. The price range lasts for twelve months.

Area D indicates the number of shares purchased between $8 and $10. The price range lasts for four months. It has been two years since the fire sale disaster.

Assume you purchased shares in this company in Area B when the shares were selling for $2.50. You bought 5,000 shares at $2.50 for $12,500. You have held the shares for twelve months and the investment is worth $30,000 at $6 a share. You **hope** that the price might recover to $10. You consult your Dead Cat Bounce manual and review the four year business cycle. You wonder what direction the market is going and where it will be in the next twelve months. You play with the two triangles on your desk. You decide that in the next six to eight months you must sell your investment before the price begins to decline.

Everyone is happy. The economy is recovering and humming along nicely. The media and the nightly business reporters are all smiles. Everything is grand. The neighbors are buying new things. The prices of gold and oil are beginning to decline. People are getting better jobs or promotions. You feel a false sense of overconfidence. You could sell 4000 shares now and leave 1000 shares to **"ride the tide."** You have held the shares for over a year and a half.

Four months later the stock is trading at $7.50. You are overjoyed. Your wife is begging you to sell. You decide to hold for another dollar or two. Rumor on the street is that the stock is on the way to $12 a share. Rumors are the same thing as lies. You wonder who would pay $7.50 a share. You realize they are first time buyers. They have finally saved enough money to buy a stock that has already doubled or almost tripled. The price has been bid up artificially. Short term traders are keeping it afloat.

The stock has resistance and trouble moving above $8. You check into your strategy room. You read the Greater Fool Theory again. The Dead Cat Bounce manual points out that you are in the D Area of the triangle. You turn the second triangle upside down over the first. Woah! You realize the stock is not going to make it to $10.

Your wife gives you the ultimatum, "If you do not sell the stock, then I am going to divorce you." Woah! You check the financials on Yahoo Finance and discover that **the income this quarter is lower than income last quarter.** Gross revenues and sales are down.

The share price *has run out of greater fools*. The profits are shrinking. The buyers have walked away and the hype is no where to be heard. The company output has dropped.

You call your discount broker and ask him to sell your shares immediately. He enters a sell order "at the market" which means that your shares will be sold **next** in front of everyone else.

The sale is made at $7.82 per share. $39,100 less the taxes.

You sold the stock! You recovered your original investment! What a wonderful profit. Your wife loves you madly. Once again you are the knight in shinning armor.

You bask in your tenacity and wisdom. You are euphoric and you want to make another trade.

You consult the Dead Cat Bounce manual and it reminds you that this specific time is a cooling off period. It will be two years before the next market disaster. Let the market go. Use the time productively to broaden investor IQ and conduct productive research. Maintain an interest and continue to monitor favorite stocks. Pay down the home mortgage and the credit cards. Look for raw land outside of town.

Your wife spends the next day reminding you that she has spent three years in a dreary kitchen that needs to be remodeled. The house needs to be painted. The second hand furniture and car that you bought to save money are falling apart and that you should quit playing the stock market while you are ahead. You just got lucky.
You remind your wife that you endure the dreariness as well. You emphasize that every cent of the profit is your money and that you will be the one to make the tough decisions. You decide to pay down the mortgage with $28,000. $11,100 remains in the brokerage account.

Use this downtime to find some low price stocks of oil and gold producers. Compile a list of both. Buy a used computer and a monthly internet service provider. Go online. Pick up one to five shares of four low price oil producers and four low price gold producers. The graphs from Securities Research Company show these companies exhibited some volatility in the last run up. Monitor them in the online brokerage account portfolio as well as the five favorite companies.

Research gold and find out that ninety eight percent of the world's gold is still in the ground. You recall some of the hype that circulated with the gold speculation. "Gold is going to $3000 an ounce." You decide to make notes and start a folder on gold with a list of all the gold mining and exploration companies from $2 to $100 that trade on the NYSE and the NASDAQ exchanges. Some of the gold exploration companies that trade in the pink sheets do not have **proven reserves** (do not bother with the pink sheets).

You tidy up your strategy area.
You make two photo copies of the two triangles. They remind you of the radioactive warning sign and the yellow caution sign. Keep one pair in your strategy folder in the desk drawer. The other pair goes on the strategy room wall next to the 100 year DJIA index wall chart from Securities Research Company. Next to the index chart is the 8.5 x 11

paper with your hand drawn graph of when the market will begin to decline. You readjust it somewhat and extend it out to the time that you believe the next fire sale disaster shopping days will occur.

One month later the stock that you sold breaks out to the $8 range on a large increase in volume. You continue to monitor. Slowly the stock begins to move to $9. **Buyers under $7 were getting out!** Short sales (not to be discussed in this book) must be coming in! The short term traders have fled. The following month the stock holds at $9 on low volume. The price finally begins to decline. Three months later the stock is back under $7.50

This is the phenomena of the Greater Fool Theory. Sell the stock by the time it moves into the D Area. When the share price gets into the D area it may be two or three times higher than it was at the beginning of the base building in Area B during the last disaster. That is good enough. You are almost two years into the recovery. If the growth demand has been met, then production will slow. Based on a four year business cycle the next two years will be in decline until the demand for goods and services increases once again.

What actually happened from Area B to Area D? The share price has been bid up similar to prices at an auction. **Everyone briefly owns the outstanding shares as the price moves up and down along the way from Area B to Area D.** The share price pattern may move back and forth between $3 and $5 in Area B two or three times before the share price pattern breaks out into Area C. Once in Area C, the share price pattern may move back and forth between $5 and $7 two or three times.

The share price pattern moves back and forth between the level of support (buyers) and the level of resistance (sellers). The share price may advance fifteen to twenty five percent (from a support level) before selling is encountered at the next resistance level (the next group of short term profit takers).

Traders take advantage of these price fluctuations. If the share price meets resistance (heavy selling), then the trader will sell and wait for the share price to fall back to the last level of support. Once the share price has dropped back to the previous support level the trader becomes a buyer again. It is possible that this pattern of opportunity will be present five or six times on the way from Area B to Area D.

The share price can pass through the resistance level and go higher if there is a steady stream of good news and the buyers out number the sellers.

Investors buy once and **hope** to sell at a higher price. Some investors will make fifty percent one time and they will buy and sell only once. A few will make a one hundred percent return on the way up and they will buy and sell only once. The important point here is that they **made it on the way up and they got out on the way up**. They did not wait until Area D. **They got out in Area C or just as the price moved into Area D.**

Traders are not concerned about taxes. They want only to make a profit. They do not want to risk holding a stock for a long period of time. **Traders do not want to lose one penny.** They are ruthless in this regard. They are willing to pay the tax on short term gains. **They are not willing to lose money on a trade.**

Mutual funds pay no tax on the short term trades they make. The gains are passed along to the mutual fund client who pays taxes if the fund shares in the individuals account are sold at a profit.

Manias

There is another possible outcome for Area D. This is something to keep in mind. Area D can be a "Mania" area. A **mania** will allow share prices to climb much higher than usual. Share prices can increase five or ten times your original investment.
$1,000 can become $10,000.

You could possibly see twenty times your money. If you recognize that a gizmo or product will take the industry by storm in the next five years, then you could see $1000 turn into $20,000 or $10,000 turn into $200,000.

A Mania can be associated with a craze or a fad. It could be the gold craze. It could be the oil jihad craze.

A mania could be a new product that opens up a whole new industry. It could be a new product that outperforms old products in an existing industry.
New products or replacement products that perform better than the old standard will eventually find acceptance.
It could be a product that adds greater efficiency to the office, the production area, the construction area, the transportation area or to the home.

A company that brings a new product to the public that is in high demand will experience growth in sales and income along with a corresponding increase in stock price for several years. UpJohn brought the birth control pill to the public market in the 1960's. The share price soared.

On occasion a mania will take the form of a large national movement. Remember the Dot Com Boom? The new generation was in. The old was on its way out.
Computers and new technology raised employee efficiency and company output. The Dot Com Boom brought the world together through the internet. The Dot Com Boom brought a new generation of investors to the stock market. They were young and savvy. The world was theirs! *The internet was going to save the world!*

A number of Dot Com companies saw share prices increase twenty times. Many investors increased their wealth. They may not have become millionaires, but they certainly made their lives much easier financially as they became debt free! Some investors made small fortunes. Some increased their wealth to over a million.

The upward move in share prices began in 1998. The NASDAQ Composite index moved from 1500 in 1998 to a whopping 4200 **in just two years. For nine months the NASDAQ Composite index remained between 3600 and 4200.** This broad long lasting spike is very impressive. There was one narrow spike to 5000 over a fifteen day period during this time.
In October of 2000, the NASDAQ began to decline. The trading volumes were phenomenal. Compare the volume in 1998 and 1999 to the volume during the downturn years 2000 and 2001.

NASDAQ COMPOSITE INDEX (COMPQ)

Broad-based market capitalization weighted methodology index

Growth Performance Measurement				
Years	Price	Earn.	Div.	Tot Ret
Last 1	43.9	-10.7	.4	44.8
Last 5	.8	4.1	8.3	1.4
Last 10	-5.7	10.1	14.6	-5.3

Bonds $.0 Mil Common .000 Mil BV $77.08 /sh P/E Ratio 26.92 Ind Ctry US

NASDAQ Composite Index

These new companies began modestly in the nineties. The companies required annual membership and purchase of software. Every year they gained more subscribers and online advertising revenue.

Every year new memberships and more product sales kept revenues increasing in large percentages compared to the previous year. The products may have been a little slow, but there was everything to like and nothing to dislike.

Everyone hears the story. The stocks become favored by investors. Netscape. AOL. Yahoo. Ebay. Microsoft. Amazon. Everyone gets on board. Everyone saves up some cash to invest. The membership growth becomes staggering to the imagination. The rest is history.

Existing companies in the computer industry participated in the Dot Com run up (Apple).

APPLE INC (AAPL)

Personal and business computer systems

Adj. for 2 for 1 6/21/00

Adj. for 2 for 1 2/28/05

(P)(E) Growth Performance Measurement				
Years	Price	Earn.	Div.	Tot Ret
Last 1	115.6	90.0	.0	115.6
Last 5	40.3	74.1	.0	40.3
Last 10	20.9	30.8	.0	20.9

Bonds $.0 Mil Common 906.795 Mil BV 34.60 /sh P/E Ratio 22.13 Ind CMPTR Ctry US

Apple

26

AMAZON COM INC (AMZN)

Retailer of books via the World Wide Web

Growth Performance Measurement				
Years	Price	Earn.	Div.	Tot Ret
Last 1	79.5	35.3	---	79.5
Last 5	30.9	16.9	---	30.9
Last 10	7.0	---	---	7.0

Audible, Inc.
acquired 3/19/08

Adj. for
3 for 1
1/5/99

(0.21) (0.53) (1.41) (1.18) (0.78) (0.09)
Adj. for (0.3 Adj. for 8) (1.37) (0.87) (0.24)
2 for 1 0.24 2 for 1 (1.48) (1.04) (0.44) 0.07
6/2/98 9/2/99

'98 '99 '00 '01 '02 '03 '04 '05 '06 '07 '08 '09 '10

Bonds $1267.0 Mil Common 444.546 Mil BV 11.84 /sh P/E Ratio 64.94 Ind RTNET Ctry US

Amazon

Look at the chart for Amazon. On the bottom horizontal axis is the trading volume and a unit of time. Each vertical line represents all of the shares traded during one month. The number of all of the shares traded is on the vertical axis at the bottom (150 million to 750 million).

The vertical axis on the right indicates the share price.

The Amazon rise was like a rocket. In January of 1998 it was trading at just above $4 a share. In six months it met resistance in the $18 area. It traded in the $18 area for five months. A large volume of shares changed hands. In November, it broke out to the $30 range. In December it was in the $50 range. The following year Amazon was in the $65 range with an occasional leap over $85.

The Amazon rise was an unusual situation. Amazon was still in the infancy stage. It was run up in share price along with the other Dot Com shares. The stock price rose by association. **The stock price made it to the stratosphere before the earnings reports arrived.**

In January of 2000, Amazon began its decline. It returned to the $5 to $7 fire sale area for three months.

If you are so fortunate to have stock trading in a mania, then you need to adjust the selling strategy. At some point you need to recover the original investment. Would you sell thirty five percent of your shares if the stock doubled or tripled in price? The other sixty five percent could be left in the market to "ride the tide?" This decision is left up to you. It is easy with hindsight.
Hopefully, every reader of the Dead Cat Bounce will be a participant in a mania someday and have to make such wonderful decisions.

What You Need To Know:
The Missouri Pacific Railroad Bonds

One beautiful summer afternoon an account executive (stockbroker) was phone canvassing (bothering people at home or work) in search of potential investors. The broker was using phone numbers obtained from a book of street listings at the library. He was "dialing for dollars" in a ritzy neighborhood. One phone call connected to a man in a wealthy neighborhood. Quite by accident a pleasant conversation began. Politely, not to be out of line, the broker asked the gentleman how he found his riches.

Here is the answer. Brace yourself.
"It was the Monday following December 7, 1941 (the Japanese attack on Pearl Harbor). The Missouri Pacific Railroad Bonds ($1,000 face value for each bond) opened for trading at $1.00 a bond. I was thirty years old. I was just out of college. I had majored in finance. I sold everything I had but my toothbrush. I was able to acquire 1500 Missouri Pacific bonds. I had to wait awhile before they recovered. It was several years, but I hung on to them."

This young man knew he could increase his wealth without risk. When World War II began the news sent the stock market tumbling down. Disaster was at the door step. The young man did not hesitate. Disaster was everywhere and he jumped in with every thing he had.

What does this tell you? Can an investor strike it rich in the stock market?

By now you know that the answer is, **"Yes!"** You will win here before you ever win the lotto. The stock market could change your life. Participate even if you begin on a small level. Get started and become familiar with this environment. Discover that **you really can win**. There is much to learn. The key is to be ready.

Find a discount broker web site that you like and open a free account. It can all be done on line over the internet. Have the social security and driver license numbers handy. Mail a deposit or arrange for wire transfer of funds between your bank and the brokerage account. Not on the net? Go to 1 800 555 1212 (toll free) information and ask for the 800 number of the discount broker.

It could be the best move you ever make.
Do not spend much money. Buy five shares of a couple of stocks. As a hobby read the news on the Ten Most Active stocks, and the Ten Most Declined stocks. Follow trends. Follow up ticks and down ticks. Continue to learn. Educate yourself.

There are new stock brokers every month beginning a career in the securities industry. Each state gives a state regulatory test for the NASD (National Association of Securities Dealers) Series Seven exam. The insurance agent candidates take only half of the exam. They are licensed in the state to sell insurance (agent) if they pass. The stock broker candidates have to take the entire test. If the broker candidates are smart, they will pay for both the insurance license and the Series Seven license.

The cram course for a Series Seven Securities License is two weeks. If you can find one, sign up for it. It will cost you some money. The candidates come from all walks of life. The average age is thirty. Some might have a bit of knowledge of the market, but for the most part these future brokers will learn the market the hard way.
This is a self help discipline. Education will get you a job. You have to find wealth by yourself. This requires persistence and desire. You already have an edge over the new brokers. You have the Dead Cat Bounce.

There is one more book to buy to "**Seal the deal.**" This book is mandatory for your success. It is the **Orange Book** from Securities Research Company.

Visit www.srcstockcharts.com on the internet. You must visit this web site. Check to ensure that indeed you are on the **Securities Research Company** web site. Their logo is "Trusted by Investors since 1933."

Click on "Chart Books." Select the Orange Book. The Orange Book consists of 1500 charts of the **most actively traded** stocks on the NASDAQ exchange.

These charts visually enhance your perception of the effect that a major market correction will have on the share prices of company stocks.

The charts from Securities Research Company

- clearly illustrate the dramatic drop of the share price of a stock during a severe market downturn.

- visually illustrate the length of time that a stock remains at the lowest price.

- visually illustrate the length of the base building period before a stock resumes an upward move.

- visually illustrate the number of shares (volume) that trade every month.

- visually illustrate the areas of resistance where selling (profit taking) is encountered.

The charts will help confirm the concept *that a steep stock market decline is the safest time to buy shares of stock.*

These charts will help you associate the main premise of this book with your fire sale shopping habits. "Buy low and sell high" is not the main premise. **The main premise of the Dead Cat Bounce is to "*Buy Disaster.*"**

The Orange Book and the Blue Book allow you to compare the day of disaster of many different companies and industries to one another.

You will begin to realize that not all 13,000 stocks can have their low point on the same day at the same time. Not all 13,000 stocks will have their low point during the low point of the DJIA index. Some industries lead the way and are the first to suffer. Some well heeled companies that pump out the product and collect the revenue drop thirty five to forty percent and recover within a month or two. Some companies bottom out after all of the others have begun to move up.

The Orange Book is vital to your success.

Do not flinch. Do not hesitate. The cost of the book is $100. For $25 more you can have the book and a three month online membership that allows you to download daily updates on many stocks that trade on the NASDAQ. Valuable technical advice from SRC is also available.

In this book you may find a stock that will continually increase in price. Find a dynamic company that will continually outperform the competition. Find one stock that you can invest in for the rest of your life.

Market Downturns

Thirty corporations make up the Dow Jones Industrial Average index. The companies have been changed at times to get rid of old dogs. Vibrant performers are required. The movement of this index must be a reflection of the direction of the 3000 companies that trade on the NYSE.

On the horizontal scale of the DJIA index graph each **year** has twelve vertical lines.
Each line represents the time element of one month. The length of the line represents the total number of shares traded in the thirty companies of the index. The length of the line (volume) is measured with the small scale on the bottom corner. The scale measurements read 100 million through 500 **million** for the DJIA Index 1 graph. The scale measurements read 3 billion through 15 **billion** for the DJIA Index 2 graph.

The vertical scale on the right side of the graph represents the index value. When the index value is graphed the index path reflects (hopefully) **the direction of the share price path of the 3000 stocks that trade on the NYSE.**

Dow Jones Industrial Average Index 1

Dow Jones Industrial Average Index 2

Look at the DJIA index **volume** in 1980 and 1981 on the horizontal scale. During these years the NYSE exchange volume for approximately 3000 stocks was 40 million shares a day. On a slow day the average number of shares traded was 20 million. The largest trading day was 90 million shares. It happened only one day each year. The large trading days occurred with the steep declines of the downturn in January, 1980 and August of 1981. The name given to this event is "panic selling." The old conventional phone lines at the brokerage firms were jammed. Investors could not reach their brokers in time to sell their stock positions.

Find the year 1987. In October, 1987, the DJIA index fell from approximately 2600 to 1650 in thirty days. Talk about disaster! Two years of mania trading and investing (1986 and 1987) were required to build the DJIA index from 1600 up to 2600.
During this precipitous decline the market dropped over four hundred points on several days. The largest trading volumes were a couple of days with 100 million shares. This might lead one to pose the question, "Does the market drop like a rock off a cliff?" The answer is, "**You bet it does!**"

The drop in October, 1987, wiped out the 1000 point index **gain made in two years of mania trading** and investing in 1986 and 1987. It was **two years after the crash** before the DJIA index made it back to the 2600 high of 1987. The 2600 DJIA index level was not seen again until **the last half of 1989.**

Shortly after the steep decline in October, 1987, the Securities Exchange Commission quickly passed a new exchange trading regulation. The law stated that after a drop of two hundred points the trading exchange would be shut down for the day. The law would **hopefully** provide time for the panic selling frenzy to cool off.

Compare the monthly trading volume in 1980 and 1981 to 1986 and 1987.
How did the volume of the number of shares increase so dramatically?

Several phenomena are responsible for the increase of the number of shares traded on a day to day basis.

- There are more international investors (individual accounts) trading in US markets.

- Computer software trading programs on the internet link investors and companies to the security dealers' floor brokers. Trades from the far corners of the world can be placed instantly when compared with the old outdated conventional telephone line services.

- Corporations have authorized and issued large amounts of common stock that has been used to acquire capital (plant, equipment, and machinery) or purchase another company. **In 1980, Exxon Corporation had 500 million shares** of outstanding stock. This was the largest amount of any American company on the NYSE. **Today, Exxon has over 1.5 billion shares** of common stock outstanding. Of course Exxon's purchase of Mobil Oil undoubtedly involved a large issue of common shares at some point. Currently, many companies on the NYSE and NASDAQ exchanges have billions of shares of common stock outstanding. CitiGroup now has **26 billion shares after the bailout**.

- Corporations increased their reserves of common stock authorized and issued the common shares to employees as contributions to retirement funds.

- The number of short term traders and the volume of short term trades increased dramatically.

- Mutual funds and brokerage houses participate in short term trading.

Here is a recent example of short term trading.
Huntington Bancshares has 716 million shares outstanding to the public. Between January, 2009 and February, 2010 over 6 billion shares have traded in the market. This is an incredible amount of short term trading.

Short term trading always existed in the market. Today it exists in an enormous way.

The stock markets consist of an enormous number of **short term traders.** These traders have one goal. That goal is to buy stocks that are moving up and sell as the stock meets resistance.

Short term traders buy and sell shares within two weeks, a week, a few days, or a few hours. They are not interested in holding a stock position longer than twelve months just to have a tax break. That would be a loss of valuable opportunities.

Short term traders play resistance levels.
Share prices rise to a resistance level where they encounter enough selling to knock the share price down five percent. Buying resumes and another upward move to the resistance level begins again. This pattern can be repetitive. If the resistance level and the trading range last for one month on an actively traded issue, then a few trades for four percent can be made.

Short term traders play disaster scenarios.
When a company has bad news the stock price will drop. As long as the company is healthy and still producing a **profit from operations** the price will recover. The most recent example is British Petroleum (BP). BP fell from $60 on the news of the Gulf oil spill. BP shares began to build a new base at $30 and have moved up towards $40.

For traders the market is not to **buy and hope**. This would be the mind set of a loser. The market exists to buy and win!

HUNTINGTON BANCSHARES INC (HBAN)

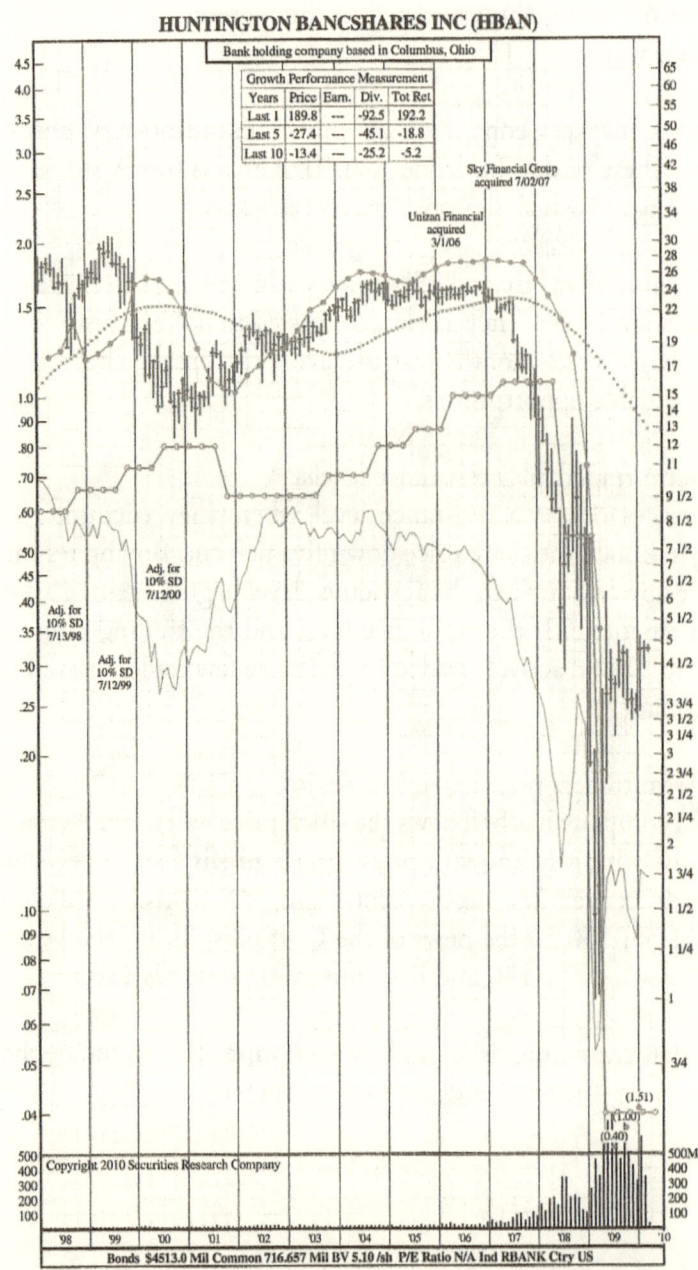

Bank holding company based in Columbus, Ohio

Growth Performance Measurement				
Years	Price	Earn.	Div.	Tot Ret
Last 1	189.8	---	-92.5	192.2
Last 5	-27.4	---	-45.1	-18.8
Last 10	-13.4	---	-25.2	-5.2

Sky Financial Group
acquired 7/02/07

Unizan Financial
acquired
3/1/06

Adj. for
10% SD
7/12/00

Adj. for
10% SD
7/13/98

Adj. for
10% SD
7/12/99

(1.51)
(1.00)
b
(0.40)

Bonds $4513.0 Mil Common 716.657 Mil BV 5.10 /sh P/E Ratio N/A Ind RBANK Ctry US

Huntington Bancshares

Return to the DJIA index chart and the years from 1982 through 1987. Ask yourself what events led up to this dramatic rise in the average. This expansion was due to a mania. It was not a mania in the sense that the Dot Com Boom was a mania. This expansion was a result of a strong belief that the market would rise.

During the stagflation years after the Viet Nam War the market was trading in a narrow range in the late 70's and early 80's. It was an opinion of many prominent brokerage firms (security dealers) that the market had lacked participation from investors in years past and that share prices did not reflect the true value of prospering companies. Wall Street and the financial communities from coast to coast **touted** that the DJIA index **was on its way to 3000!** Perhaps this was optimistic, but after all, the market had been held back in the 70's and early 80's. A good announcement (rumor) was needed to get the market back into action. The sentiment on the street was that share prices would climb and the DJIA index would soon be on the way to 3000.

The consolidation or rebuilding phase for the thirty companies that comprise the DJIA index is approximately six months. The actual recession will last a year or more.

October and Black Friday

It takes a long time to close the books at the end of a year. **The end of the fourth business quarter and the business calendar year is June 30.** This is a good time to close out the end of the year as there are no back to back holidays (Thanksgiving, Christmas, and New Years) to interrupt this extensive project. There is barely enough time at the end of the civilian calendar year (your normal civilian year end December 30) to get the 1099s and the W2s printed up for the employees.

The financial statements must be approved and closed for the year by the BOD (Board of Directors).
A company audit is performed by an independent group of auditors.
The auditors review the company records. They affirm that the financial statements are ninety eight percent accurate.

Summation of the data for the entire year is compared to the year end data of the previous two to four years in the annual report for the shareholders and potential investors. Hopefully, this comparison reflects a pattern of increased sales and revenues. An increase in sales and revenues has a positive effect on the share price.

The first fiscal (business) quarter of the **corporate year** is July, August and September. It ends September 30. When September 30 passes the results of the **first** quarter financial statements are completed.

It seems as if nothing is going on in the markets during August and September. Everyone has forgotten about the stock market. Parents are getting ready to get the kids back to school. Everyone is saving the money for the upcoming holidays Thanksgiving and Christmas. It appears no one really cares what is going on in the markets.

Folks, you can bet your waders that the serious short term traders are trying to find out the results of the first quarter reports. Make no mistake. The decision to sell or "lighten up" is being made at this juncture.

The thrust of all the concern is this.
Is the company is moving ahead in sales, revenues and income? Is it ahead of the last quarter and the first quarter of the previous year? Is it ahead of the competition?

This news will in fact have an effect on which way the share price will move.
Investors are chomping at the bit. Good news and good news only keeps stocks poised at their current price. Bad news will send stocks lower.

The reports must reflect at minimum that the company is holding steady or advancing with regard to profit and production. Anything less than that will culminate in a five percent or greater decline of the share price as these announcements become public. You can bet an eraser all of the chief operating officers of every department will lose their skin if this year is not better than last.

In the case of the economic and growth doldrums the company may be losing profit and production may be shrinking. If the year is down and the first quarter is down at the end of September 30, then the short term traders will sell. They will check the revenue and earnings reports of companies in the same industries to determine if an industry wide slowdown exists. If there is not an industry wide slowdown, then they will look for shares in companies that are reporting better revenues and earnings.

Investors will wait to see if the effect is small or large on the common share price. If the price backs off a bit but holds, then investors and short term traders become buyers. If the price continues to drop, then this will precipitate more selling. The shares will slide ten to fifteen percent.

If the company financials are compiled on the regular calendar year, then September 30, will be the end of the third quarter. Investor concern remains the same. In the next three months will the company surpass last years performance?

October is the month where all of this innuendo is taking place. The market reacts accordingly to the **facts, lies, and rumors** of the time. If the news is bad, then October reacts with short term buyers turning into sellers. If the news is good, then short term buyers invest in shares moving up. If the market stays healthy, then the market may advance through the second quarter and the Thanksgiving and Christmas holidays.

October is often a rough month because of this scrutiny. If buyers and sellers draw the conclusion that prices are in a downtrend by the end of the first quarter, September 30, then the share price drop occurs in October. If the entire economy and market is in a downturn, then Black Friday appears!

Are you a buyer or a seller? You are both. It would be great to buy and have the share go up forever, but it does not always work that way. We have to be buyers and sellers based upon what we see happening and what we know from the past.

Thin Ice

The Dead Cat Bounce makes assumptions and generalizations in order to facilitate learning. The next three pages will be repetitious in order to communicate the phenomena and the intricacies of the "**fire sale environment**." Professional analysts, chartists and other associated disciplines may not be in agreement with the descriptions or the terminology. Please be tolerant. The reader will find correct terminology as time goes on.

When you are **fire sale shopping** while walking on thin ice it is necessary to watch the volume and price movement. Keep a record so you can compare the stock price moves to the previous days and weeks. Use the **"window"** to chart the path.

A share price will fluctuate during the trading day. It may go up or down a few cents to the next trade. The share price will fluctuate up and down in a normal range of one to two percent of the total share price. Sometimes the range is two to four percent. We are going to refer to this range as the **"window."**

For example a $10 dollar stock will fluctuate during the trading day in a small range of (say arbitrarily) twenty five to thirty five cents. It is usually trading at $10 but one day it might be down thirty five cents and the next day it might be up thirty five cents.

Track this window. A path will appear that will indicate if the share price is advancing or declining. In fire sale disaster shopping, track the stocks to the lowest share price. At that point you have to determine if the price is holding and building a base from which the share price can move up without encountering sellers.

When you track a share price to the bottom of the crash it is best to use graphs that have the volume of shares **expressed in weeks or days** on the horizontal axis. This is easily done on the discount broker websites and Yahoo Finance. They have graphs of one trading day and five trading days. Print the graphs of the week out so you can review the trading price window and volume every day of the week. Keep the weeks in order. Now you have the price pattern every day in a row for a month.

If the price down ticks on **more volume**, large volume or no volume, then you are on **thin ice**. The price will go lower.

If the share price path has remained in the same area on small volume, large volume or no volume, then the shares may have built a base support level.
The shares may be at the lowest price the share will experience.
With more up ticks than downticks on little volume, no volume or more volume, then the share price path will be moving up from this base building (support level) in a convincing manner.

Here is a pattern you need to remember. **The price moves up on little or no volume.** This is a good sign that there is demand for the stock. This is what to look for. **Determine that the large selling has finished.**
Up ticks on little volume occasionally indicate a forthcoming announcement of good news. This is also an indication that buyers have returned and are willing to risk at this time. They are betting that the price path is going to go up and they are willing to pay the higher share price.
To be a winner, buy shares that are moving up.
You are going to be a winner.

Caution is needed. This is the "**Thin Ice**" phase. *You could lose fifty percent of your money* very quickly. The bottom of the market is not a bad time to have a gamble reverse, but remember that *the ice can break twice.* There are very often two drops in share price of fifty percent or more as a stock closes in on the low point.

The message here is to be on the safe side the first time you go fire sale shopping! Watch for the base building support phase. The window may still fluctuate, but there should be **no more declines other than a few small down ticks**.
Wait to make certain the price holds and that it holds on volume increases with an up tick.
Most conservative **fire sale shoppers** wait four weeks to be on the safe side.

The shortest waiting period to determine that a stock has bottomed out and that it has gained support is two weeks.
To buy immediately after two weeks of no further decline is tempting and it can pay off with a larger return; however, you will be at risk. You will be taking more risk than you need to. It is impossible to know this is will be the lowest share price. If you buy, then please **commit only one fourth of your funds or less.** Should the stock drop another fifty percent from $3 to $1.50 or $1 to fifty cents place another one fourth of the funds at the new low price. The best thing to do is wait for the third week or at least until Thursday of the third week. If the stock jumps, up a quarter or fifty cents, then that is the sign to commit. Go for it.

Citigroup (C) was at a dollar for less than two weeks. If you jumped into the fire and bought it at $1 in the first week that the ice broke for the second time and it fell from $3 to $1, then you doubled your gambling money. If you were watching but did not buy at $1 then you could have bought at $1.50 or $2 as it moved back to $3. A fifty percent return on a gamble in that very short period of time is **excellent!** This is the goal!

You win whether 1000 or 10,000 shares are purchased! Be proud. Never fell defeated or frustrated. Never feel disappointed that investing in a stock is useless or not enough of a gain. Be proud. Be gratified that your selection and timing is correct.

What matters here is that you develop new skills that can be used again. Develop the skill to track share prices to the low point. Respect the interim period to ensure that the share price path is up. Develop the judgment for the correct time to purchase shares. This is a major accomplishment. Be proud of this accomplishment and pursue this endeavor with enthusiasm. Change your life financially.

As you go through this six to nine month phase of bottom fishing take notes. Record thoughts and print the graphs of the stocks you follow along with any good advice filtered from other sources. This will be valuable reference material for your next ice walk.

In disaster fire sale shopping it is possible to buy and sell with fifty to one hundred percent profits more than once. After you have been through one down turn and witnessed the phenomena, you might be able to get two pure plays the next time.
You will be surprised at how many times you could have made more than one play.

OK. Now just because you found the bottom does not mean you can grab the channel changer or take off on a vacation. The base building phase is what the fire sale shoppers are watching for. A stock moving up from $1.25 to $2 will move to $3 much faster. This is a sure sign the buyers are back. If you have the channel changer in your hand you will miss it.

Watch for **a reverse in market direction**. This reverse is known as the **"double dip"** recession. There may be four to six months of **solid market base building** (low point). There may be a convincing broad market share price move from this consolidation that will last for three to four months possibly even a year.
However, if the recovery dries up and falters, then the market will weaken and fall back. If earnings reports are losing ground and the market begins to weaken and decline, then sell your positions. Watch as a stock moves to a higher level to see if the selling resistance encountered is remaining small. Down ticks must be small and they may occur occasionally, but downticks should not be linked one to another (day after day). They should be interspersed with up ticks and there should be a greater balance of up ticks than downticks.

Selection

The environment that has been outlined and described in the last forty six pages is **the bottom of a severe stock market decline.** The parameters and the atmosphere have been outlined. The assumptions and concepts have been presented to you.

By now you know that **the heart of disaster** is much different than "Buy low and sell high."

Disaster is the lack of a heartbeat in the emergency room. The market must be revived. Disaster begs the application of the paddles because there are no more buyers. Disaster begs that share prices be dropped in order to find a price where buyers and sellers will begin to trade.

This method of *investing in disaster* has been used successfully by many investors over the last seventy years. Of all the strategies to make a profit in the market, investing in disaster is the best. **It is not fool proof.** The correct time and the correct company selection is what will determine your success. *The author can not be held liable for bad selection or bad timing on the part of the reader.*

Now it is time to put a little perspective on **the selection of a good company**.

A good physician will study the medical history of a patient and run some tests to determine the existence of an illness.

An investor can diagnose a company by running some tests on financial statements.

Develop the ability to analyze financial statements. An investor with this ability will select healthy companies. The ones with illness will be avoided.

The current assets ratio, the current liabilities ratio, the inventory ratio, operating margins, fixed ratio, and the working capital ratio will tell an investor if the company is performing poorly due to inefficient operation or losing market share to the competition.
Analysis will reveal if the company is an ongoing concern or if it is just a matter of a few months before the company has to close its doors. The ratios are simple math.

At first it may seem that you are overwhelmed with detail, but with just a little bit of skull sweat you will be ready for the emergency room on disaster day. You will pick out the good companies and leave the bad ones alone. The bad ones may be the last to recover.

Here is an example.
Let's say you are **fire sale shopping** in the *disaster* environment. You have been watching several robust company stocks that are down forty to fifty percent from their highs of last year. They are your favorite picks.
The share price of one company not on your watch list has fallen eighty percent! Wow! You could make a bundle if that baby recovers in a year. The stock is under $5.
If the company is in financial trouble **it may not produce a Dead Cat bounce. The ice, however, will keep breaking** time and time again as the company may be headed out of business or into bankruptcy. **You will lose your hard earned money.**

For instance,
CitiGroup would have gone into bankruptcy at one dollar a share or less **if the government had not bailed them out.** The shares would have been suspended from trading on the exchange. In this instance if you

play a hunch and purchase CitiGroup at $3 or $1 a share, then you may have money tied up in a bankruptcy for a year or more. If the company goes out of business, then you lose your **hard earned dollars** due to a worthless stock selection. **You would miss other opportunities**.

Even if the company emerges from bankruptcy there is no guarantee that it will be an ongoing concern or that the stock price will recover.

Most investors were keenly aware that the Federal Government would bailout the banking industry. This reduced the risk of purchasing the shares of CitiGrooup.

A troubled company will not see an upward share price move. If it does, then it will be the last stock out of 13,000 to move. **It will be a dog**. The investor will watch with regret as everything else begins to move. The dog will not provide any price appreciation. Other opportunities will be missed if you are holding a dog for a month or two. Sell the dog. Take the loss.

If a company drops fifty percent in share price **in the first two years of an economic expansion** there could be several reasons.

- The product is not competitively priced.
- The product is no longer desirable.
- High operating, manufacturing and administrative expenses.
- Not a durable product.
- Old inefficient plant.
- Old inefficient management.
- Low worker wages.
- Poor employee work.
- Too large to operate efficiently.
- Can not meet a bond obligation at the bond's maturity date (or other current liability).
- Accidents and loss of property.
- Lawsuits and product liability.

A corporation that can not meet a bond obligation at the bond's maturity date is a corporation that has a financial problem. This is a corporation that is in trouble no matter how big or what wonderful product it produces.

If the company can arrange a satisfactory agreement with the bond holders to use common shares in an amount equivalent to make up for the lack of cash payment (or another arrangement), then they have dodged a bullet temporarily.

Investors must avoid bad selection.

Now it is your turn!
You are the one who must become pro active. Immerse yourself in this environment. **You** must become the one to *explore the pathways*. **You** must become the one to *make the discovery.*
The disaster environment is the ideal time for you to profit.
Once potential and novice investors have witnessed a steep decline in stock prices first hand, then they are in agreement to buy stocks at the bottom of the market.

You should be more than agreeable. Your main agenda should be to enter a steep market decline and discover the environment and the pathways.

Throw away the channel changer and the action games. Leave the stale environment. The TV is only going to burn out on you and you with it.

Instead of watching a dreary reality TV show, pick up the phone and pursue the entry into the world of wealth. Empower yourself to make decisions to bring you wealth instead of which channel or movie to watch.

Before you put this book down open a **free** account with a discount broker on the internet (Charles Schwab, AmeriTrade, Etrade, Scott Trade). Take the first step. You will be amazed.

Find a corner in one room to set up a strategy table. You will feel good about yourself when you get to this point. Order the Securities Research Company Orange Book. Between the front and back cover 1500 graphs await your scrutiny. This book will be an inspiration. The first day you look at the graphs you will find more than ten companies that will keep you moving forward with this new vocation.

In thirty days you will have one to five shares in five companies in different industries. Eventually you will become comfortable with this ongoing learning experience. Thirty days pass. Six months pass. Move from novice to beginner and on to intermediate.
A year goes by. Being a spectator on the sidelines or watching reality TV and Oprah is no longer an option. Enjoy being part of your own reality. Make a one hundred and eighty degree turn in your active financial life.

Become involved and excited one day at a time. Answer the questions "What should I do next?" or "What needs to be done?" This is called problem solving. It does not matter that you do not have the solution immediately. Think about it. You will figure out a couple of alternative views or solutions. Answers will come to you in the next day or two.

College and Trade schools will get you a job. To find wealth you must educate yourself. Only your own drive, your own will and desire and your own dogged pursuit will bring you wealth.

Appendix

Your Home Mortgage

Somewhere around the age of forty many of us become complacent with what we have. We no longer push ourselves or work as hard. Our attitudes and work ethic begin to fade along with our hopes and dreams. We decide to take the take the middle of the road and we begin to coast. My friend, do not become complacent. Trust me. This is not a good idea.

At the age of fifty, your burdens include more variables. You may not want to work as hard. Financially, the kids and the grand children need your help now and then. If the house is not paid off, you realize that you will be working full time to the age of sixty and beyond.

If the mortgage was refinanced to pay off credit cards and other expenses, then the monthly payments are twice as high as the original payments. If you are a victim of a collapsed economy and are laid off from the job, then you may go into foreclosure on the mortgage and lose the house. **The appreciation in the value of the home** will disappear along with more than **one third of the monthly income for the last twenty years**. Mortgage companies do not give credit for twenty years of loyalty. They merely put you into foreclosure. What a terrible time to realize that you will not be able to retire at the age of sixty. Life is truly wonderful but financially there are struggles at every turn.

Make no mistake about it. The home is the most important investment.

The safest financial investment you can make is to pay down a thirty year mortgage in fifteen years. **This is an important concept**.

To pay off the house in fifteen years is a terrific savings plan. You realize a savings of approximately ninety thousand dollars or more in mortgage interest on a one hundred and fifty thousand dollar house. Think of it as making ten times your money over ten years on a $9,000 investment in the stock market.

Remember, if the house is paid off, then you can survive a job lay off. You can take a lower paying job and still survive financially. You will not lose the house or have to sell it. If the value of the home goes down, **who cares**? It is paid for! You can live for free! No one believes they will ever experience a job lay off.

Good paying jobs are sometimes the first to go. Visualize paying down the principle balance on the home three thousand to five thousand dollars every year!

Does that mean you have to give up the retirement account?

If the chart of your employer's stock has a lack luster performance and there is nothing hot in the hopper, then the answer is yes. Yes for the simple reason that if the house has been refinanced and it is not paid off in thirty years, then it will break your financial back. Get the house paid off! Afterward you can open an IRA.

If your employer has a retirement plan you will be asked to view the power point presentation. You may be in a group of recently hired workers. The presentation will introduce the IRA plan. The usual presentation will explain when and how much the company will contribute to the retirement account. The company stock may be offered at a price lower than it currently trades on the open market. Your monetary contribution of $1,000 to $5,000 is usually converted to shares of company stock at a discount price. In later years your contribution is matched to some degree by the company.

A form letter is passed around to be filed out. You are supposed to indicate how much money you want to contribute to the IRA account from the monthly paycheck.

Now is the time to be bold. Be audacious. Tell the host that you are planning on making a $5,000 payment to reduce the principle amount of the home mortgage this year. Ask the host if the company will match the principle reduction payment that you will make on the home mortgage. There are companies that do this.

Tell them you prefer to pay down the mortgage because there is **no risk**. The dollar amounts are set in stone and the hard earned money is not subject to the drifting prices of the stock market.

The employer may argue that the value of the home may decrease. You remind them of three things.

- If the home is paid off, then you can live there for free and have all of the money from the monthly paycheck.
- Remind them that you will save ninety thousand dollars if you pay the mortgage off in fifteen years.
- Remind them that you can not live under a pile of worthless stock certificates.

The host may look at you as if you are crazy. He or she may perform an impressive tap dance of double talk and gibberish. This dance is designed to overcome the objections.

Then the spokesperson will ask you intimidating questions linked to high finance. Basically, they believe that the company stock will never go down. The best answer to these intimidating financial questions should be, "Will it save me ninety thousand dollars? Will you put that in writing?" If the host dances away from the original question by changing the subject, or if he expresses a look of shock or anger, then speak up and remind him in a loud voice that, **"Debt is the most common failure to the individual."**

If you are so lucky as to be in a dynamic company and the stock is on its way to the moon, then select the stock for the retirement account. If the stock is a dog in the doldrums, then sell it and leave the proceeds in the account for a better opportunity.

Never stop learning and never give up. You are going to learn how to build your financial wealth and not lose it.

Your Ira Or Keogh

The company power point presentation. Looks pretty good, doesn't it? The price to pay for shares of company stock in the IRA may be lower than the current market price.

Management believes the price of their stock will continue to climb in the long run. Play along with them. Graphs over long periods of time give the impression that the market is always going up. The small downturns look temporary. Rest assured the small downturns were due to recessions or a decrease in company production. Rest assured that the share price of the company stock took a nose dive as well.

The company may offer extra stock because you have been a conscientious worker for five years. If the time and price happens to be in Area B, **then you are a winner!**

The company will have an in house retirement plan department or an arrangement with a securities representative. Contact this entity and check to make certain that you have control of buying and selling in your account.

If you are in Area D then sell the shares and leave the cash proceeds in the account. If it is a large amount of money, then take the money out and pay down the home mortgage. There will be an early withdraw penalty. The prepaid penalty will be made up in the reduction of the heavy interest payments on the mortgage principle. The day you do not have to send **one third of the monthly income** to the mortgage company **will arrive ten years early.**
This action would be preferable to holding the stock during a two year market decline. Who wants to watch stock in a retirement account sink fifty percent in value over two years?

What if the IRA is up to eighty thousand dollars from the contributions for the last ten to fifteen years and then the IRA **collapses fifty percent?**

You will never make up this loss. This is gambling and you lost with hard earned money. What could be worse? Seventy five percent would be worse.

You are responsible for your gain. Lock in the gain. Sell! Call the portfolio manager and convert the shares to cash! The only way to realize profit in an IRA or a mutual fund is to sell before the value drops. If the business cycle has expanded two years and right now the GNP and the stock market are going sideways and slipping down, then sell. Do this **because you are a winner**. Do not listen to other people's baloney or hang along for the ride. "Suffer no fools." If the stock continues to go up, there will always be another time. Count on a stock market collapse in the fourth year *maybe fifty percent of the time*.
If it does not happen in the fourth year it will by the sixth. On average there is at least one **severe** market decline every ten years.

Is it better to invest in the stock market, the IRA or the home mortgage? Which is more important? They are all important. The main point here is that the money is hard earned money. Your hard earned money should not be lost in a stock market gamble.

If the employer stock falls fifteen to twenty five percent an analyst for the company may print up a recommendation not to sell the stock.
"Hold on to the stock. In the long run the stock will recover! The stock will outperform the competition. Good news is coming!"
A month later the analyst will announce some dreary little news that is common knowledge.
After two years of reading recommendations and research one understands that "Hold" means that **the stock is a dog**. It will recover after many investors more important than you sell their shares first (brokerage firms and mutual funds).

If there is an impending across the board economic downturn, sell the shares. If you are a millionaire, then hang on. If you were not losing your job and going into foreclosure you could hang on.
If the company is leading the competition in sales of gizmos, then the investment might be safe.

Management may talk about insider trading. They will say in some instances you may not be able to sell the shares in the IRA account.

Announcements will cause a company stock to rise.
- a lucrative contract
- a large increase in net earnings or revenues
- a pending merger
- an acquisition
- an announcement of a miracle cure
- an announcement of a new product that will beat the competition

If you have knowledge of such information and pass this to an individual who does not, then you may become part of the violation. The general public does not have access to this information.
If the individual buys the shares before the announcement and then sells them at a profit after the stock moves up, then they have benefited monetarily.
This chain of events is known as insider trading and both people are guilty at any point in the process.
Otherwise, sell the employee shares anytime.

The concept of IRA and the Keogh plans was designed to encourage people to increase their savings and invest for their retirement.
The plans were enacted into law through congress with good intentions. Hopefully, it would be a solution to the coming social security crisis. More people could manage their own retirement and their employers could help. Companies and individuals would no longer have to pay social security taxes. What a sales job!

Stocks do not always go up. Citigroup employee retirement plans are at an all time low.
The employees at Enron lost all of the value in their retirement shares. Retirement shares at banks that have closed are worthless. Bank shares that have dropped from $20 a share to $3 have lost the worker's hard earned money.

Obviously, the main attraction of the IRA or Keogh is the capital gains income tax advantage. **There are no taxes on the gains made in the stock market in the IRA or Keogh account.** The tax exempt ploy was used deliberately to influence individuals to consider the retirement plans. Government sometimes has a slick way of selling ideas to the to the public. Consumer decisions are influenced if government makes something taxable or tax exempt.

Regardless, everyone hopped on the retirement wagon!

Mutual Funds

Here is a brief summary of the last 40 years of mutual fund history. The following figures are approximate. They are not exact.

In 1969 there were 250 mutual funds in the USA. After the market crash in 1970 there were 25 mutual funds that survived the crash. The others closed up shop as fast as ice cream melts on a hot summer day. In 1977 there were approximately 2500 mutual funds. After the market crash in 1978 there were 250 mutual funds that were financially sound and able to continue in business.

Today there are over 30,000 mutual funds in the world.

The mutual fund expansion began after the IRA and Keogh plans became law. Mutual funds became the preferred investment vehicle for retirement accounts.

Investors wanted an investment method that would bring them some worthwhile gains rather than the meager money market profits. Self employed individuals looked to mutual funds for their retirement accounts. It was considered the astute thing to do. A team of knowledgeable professionals could increase your wealth.

Your money is in the hands of professional managers. Some of them are armed with the most sophisticated trading software programs in the world. Relax. You do not have to be directly involved with the trading decisions. The fund managers buy and sell stocks to increase the value of the fund. Their gains are reflected by the increase in the value of your fund shares. Sit back and watch the investment grow. Ride it all the way to the top of the market **and then make a decision to sell.** Mutual funds do not magically continue to rise. Mutual funds are subject to the same uncertainties and market fluctuations as shares of company stock.

The share value is the current price you will receive **if you sell the shares.** Profit is not "realized" or "locked in" until the shares are sold.

You are responsible to contact the mutual fund account representative or company sponsor. Sell the fund shares and realize the gain.

After the 2009 crash a few funds are up as much as two hundred percent within a year. Astute managers who anticipated the downturn sold part of the fund's investments (hopefully at a profit) to raise cash. They **waited for the thin ice to break and then they went fire sale shopping.**
If you invest in a mutual fund do some homework. Check the reputation and the credentials of the fund and the managers. Forbes magazine rates the performance of mutual funds.

If there is a corruption factor of one percent or more in the industry then three hundred funds out of thirty thousand may be fraudulent. Everyone has heard of Bernie Madoff. There are pyramid schemes in the world to steal your money. You may remember Michael Milliken the Junk Bond King.

The account executives are perceived as knowledgeable veterans of the stock market. They appear to be confident survivors of the last market calamity.
They have a propensity to brag and swagger. They have some hot air to blow up pants and skirts. "Our funds have returned seventeen percent every year for the last five years. It will pay for the children's college education. We are ranked in the top twenty five mutual funds in the nation and the top fifty in the world. We have conservative funds. We have highly diversified funds. We have businessman's risk funds and world growth funds." They add with a whisper, "Our funds gained more than ten percent in the last market crash."
Account executives believe the fund value will never go down.

Do You Have What It Takes To Win?

To realize a gain in the market is exciting. Eventually, the euphoria will wear off and you can go on with life as if nothing happened. The memory of the win will linger.

You will be eager to repeat your success. Fire sale disaster opportunities are fleeting. They are not available every day. Investors do their shopping every three years or so.

It is just as easy to lose your money chasing stocks. The euphoria and the fast money can keep investors addicted to look for a win. If investors become reckless with their purchases (playing a hunch) and the share price goes down, then they will have to sell at a loss. After several bad selections the available funds will have evaporated into thin air.

Be careful if you want to experiment with the trading environment. Use a small amount of money to explore greater risks. Investing a small amount of money keeps a lively atmosphere. Win or lose the risk taken is more likely to be remembered. Gains from investments when the market is in a two year decline are more difficult to capture. Do not bet the family fortune when trading outside of the disaster environment.

It is important to follow the market during market declines.
Staying current assures the ability to act with knowledge. Do not become greedy. You do not have to trade every week or every month. Be patient and gain the perspective of an opportunist. The opportunities will appear before you. Recognize them and take advantage of the situation. Check your stocks at least once a week. Browse the Orange Book for stocks that you want to research and track.

When the economy has recovered and the NYSE and NASDAQ **stocks are closing on their highs**, then oil stocks should be dropping in price along with gold. Gold and oil shares eventually drop in price because their earnings have been in decline. The whole world has cut back on usage. Entities have built up stock piles. Demand is no longer at a high level.

When oil slips back under $60 dollars a barrel for **six months to a year** the sales revenues on the income statement will be much lower than they were when the commodity was over $140 a barrel. The share price will fall. Study the cycles and the length of time the commodity is at the low price. Research back two decades or more. Accumulate some shares for the long haul. Then wait for the day that the next run up begins. You will have a long term gain with oil and with gold.

No one knows for certain if oil or gold will fall back to the same price as before their respective run ups. New discoveries of oil or gold will increase supply and cause prices to return to their previous lows or lower. The North Pole has oil. The ability and cost to retrieve oil in the polar region will certainly be an expensive test.

Watch the large brokerage firms for the "touts" on emerging growth companies. When "the Street" backs a cause or finds a darling, then the street will get behind the darling and move it up in share price.

Watch for touts on existing companies that are expanding to take more market share.
AIG a large insurance concern began at $2 a share. There is bound to be an existing insurance company that is dreaming of replacing AIG. There is bound to be a new product that is better or more efficient than the existing ones.

Watch for the growth company.
Follow any industry or company that is beating the competition and know the reasons why they are ahead. These stocks will continue to advance during the first year of the two year market decline.

The securities dealers will bring "initial public offerings" to the investing public.
The IPOs are advertised over the internet and through the business news on brokerage web sites. Be very careful.
They may be new start ups or they may be successful privately held companies that have been producing for five years or longer. The new start ups may allow enormous sales of insider stock (rule 144 stock or

other restricted stock) at some time after the shares are trading publicly (dilution). Occasionally there are incredibly large numbers of insider shares released. This will cause the public share price to plummet.

Take advantage of any singular company accidents or incidents. Unfortunate incidents will cause a share price to fall.

Many times an incident will not affect the sales revenues for the quarter. Exaggerated media and news headlines will initiate selling. Would be buyers hold off on purchase of the shares. When there are no buyers the share price will fall.

You know this environment and scenario. This is a low risk opportunity for a short term gain as long as the company is still showing operating profits.

Just as in the **Thin Ice** period, wait until the price is building a base. Determine that the selling is over. Wait for the shares to begin to advance before you buy.

BP with the Gulf Oil Spill disaster is the current classic example.

Get factual reporting. The best factual business news in the local and global business world is through your internet brokerage site. The emotional reporting on the TV stations is slanted.

Be wary of all of the independent newsletters and investment advisors associated with analysis or predictions of stock performance. You do not need them. You have the Orange Book.

Many of the newsletter recommendations are already up as much as fifteen to twenty five percent because the recommendations are leaked (front running). By the time the average investor has the list the first round of short term traders are taking profits and the list drops twenty percent.

Usually the recommendations will drop fifteen to twenty five percent before they rally back and net a return of twenty to forty percent.

Research at the library is a break from staying at home with the internet. Not all the answers are on the internet and sometimes the answers are not complete.

Search your notes for all of the unanswered questions and interests that you want to research. The business section in the library is a good place. Some business departments have current annual reports and valuable reference books with financial and operational detail on companies.

Read up on **the power of the corporation.** Corporations have their own laws, their own lawyers, and their own printing presses (common stock and bonds). College level accounting or finance books will introduce you totally to the financial statement and ratio analysis. Research the instruments in shareholders equity and liabilities. Corporate debt and financing is something you should understand. Learn as much as possible about the corporate environment.

If you are caught up on what interests you have, and have nothing else to do, then research the gold rush from 1850 through 1933 and the relation that gold and US dollars once had. Investigate the beginning of American Smelting and Refining Company (ASARCO and the Guggenheim fortune). Learn of the Federal intervention in 1893 and the bust to zero for silver.

Gain some knowledge of the costs of hard rock mining at depths greater than two thousand feet. How much does it really cost to recover one ounce of gold from one ton of mineral ore in a hard rock mine at a depth of 2000 feet as opposed to placer mining? What are proven reserves? How big are reclamation costs?

Research the oil industry from the early fields in Oklahoma. Read about the formation of Standard Oil and Continental Oil (CONOCO). How many shares were issued in the original formation of the companies? How much money was contributed by the major share holders, officers, and directors?
How much does ocean floor platform drilling cost?

What will bring you wealth? Your **desire** and your **drive** will bring you wealth.
Your self education will bring you wealth.

About the Author

Bill Overmyer worked as a stockbroker in Denver, Colorado. He witnessed three devastating market downturns. After several attempts to share his experience with potential investors he decided to write an easily understood guide that would lead a new investor safely through the paths of a stock market disaster. Bill lives in Colorado where he enjoys camping and skiing in the Rocky Mountains.